FACT FRENZY

PLANET EARTH

CONTINENTS

Lisa Regan

PowerKiDS press

Published in 2020 by **The Rosen Publishing Group, Inc.**
29 East 21st Street, New York, NY 10010

Cataloging-in-Publication Data

Names: Regan, Lisa.
Title: Continents / Lisa Regan.
Description: New York : PowerKids Press, 2020. | Series: Fact frenzy: planet Earth | Includes glossary and index.
Identifiers: ISBN 9781725395435 (pbk.) | ISBN 9781725395459 (library bound) | ISBN 9781725395442 (6 pack)
Subjects: LCSH: Continents--Juvenile literature.
Classification: LCC G133.R43 2020 | DDC 910.914'1--dc23

Manufactured in the United States of America

CPSIA Compliance Information: Batch CSPK20: For Further Information contact Rosen Publishing, New York, New York at 1-800-237-9932.

Contents

FACT 1

AFRICA IS GOING TO RIP IN TWO

The movement of Earth's plates has created an enormous rift valley across part of Africa, known as the East African Rift. The crust is being stretched, and the eastern part of Africa will eventually split away from the rest of the continent.

On the move

Our continents haven't always looked the way they do today. About 225 million years ago, there was just a single, large landmass known as Pangaea. This "supercontinent" gradually broke apart into separate continents. The theory of continental drift was first put forward by a German named Alfred Wegener (1880–1930) in the early 20th century. He proposed that the existence of mountain ranges at the edge of plates suggested that the plates were moving and colliding.

NORTH AMERICA AND EUROPE ARE MOVING APART AT ABOUT 1 INCH (2.5 CM) PER YEAR.

Dino clues

Wegener offered other evidence to support his theory. He noted how the shapes of South America and Africa fit together like jigsaw pieces. He also pointed out that similar fossils are found across the continents, even though they are now so far apart. During the Triassic Period, for example, an ancestor of Spinosaurus lived on the supercontinent, and left fossil evidence in both Africa and South America.

Extra evidence

One thing Wegener could not explain was how the plates moved. It took many more years, and several geologists, to do this. Mapping the ocean floor with radar technology, they discovered mid-ocean ridges and seafloor spreading, which gave scientists the evidence they needed to propose that the plates moved around on a layer of semi-molten rock beneath the crust.

THE PYGMY MARMOSET IS A NEW WORLD MONKEY, ORIGINATING FROM THE AMERICAS.

Joined apart

Geographers divide the world's landmasses into seven continents, but they are not all clearly separated. North and South America are joined together and are often termed the "New World" by biologists when giving labels to species. Europe and Asia are a single, enormous landmass, but culturally are quite different. Geographers usually include nearby islands as part of a continent, such as Japan, which is in Asia.

FACT 2 BANGKOK IS HOTTER THAN THE SAHARA

Bangkok, in Thailand, is officially the world's year-round hottest city, with temperatures regularly above 104°F (40°C). They stay this high even at night, and the humidity is also high, making life here hot and sticky.

FACT 3 The two wettest towns are both in India, and receive around 36 feet (11 m) of rain per year.

Hot spots

It can be hard to know which are the hottest places on Earth. Most of them are so inhospitable that it is impossible to set up recording equipment. However, NASA satellites can be used to check surface temperatures. The highest confirmed reading came from the Lut Desert in Iran, at 159.3°F (70.7 °C). Australia's Badlands are close behind, at 156.7°F (69.2°C), but many African locations, including the Sahara, regularly reach over 104°F (40°C) in the daytime.

AUSTRALIA IS OFFICIALLY THE DRIEST INHABITED CONTINENT ON THE PLANET.

No sweat

Many of the world's hottest places are also dry. Bangkok is different because of its humidity (the amount of moisture held in the air). If there is a lot of water, then humidity is high, and it is hard for our bodies to lose heat by sweating. Lower humidity helps sweat to evaporate, keeping us cooler even in high temperatures.

FACT 4

Smells are more easily detected in a humid environment; that's why some humid cities smell pretty bad.

The desert city of Las Vegas is one of the least humid cities in the US.

Damp and dry

Humidity is not the same as rainfall. Although moisture can condense into clouds and fall as rain, that isn't always the case. Arica in Chile is comparatively humid, but still receives less than 0.4 inch (1 cm) of rain per year. Measured by rainfall, it is the world's driest inhabited place.

Subzero

While high temperatures are rarely recorded by human observers, cold ones are much better known. Antarctica has no towns or cities, but does have research stations where temperatures as low as -128.6°F (-89.2°C) have been noted. At the opposite end of the globe, places in the Arctic Circle also see the thermometer drop to -90°F (-68°C), with Russia staking claim to the coldest towns in the world.

THE RUSSIAN CITY OF VERKHOYANSK HAS THE GREATEST TEMPERATURE RANGE ON EARTH: FROM -89°F (-67°C) IN WINTER TO 99°F (37°C) IN SUMMER.

FACT 5 ANTARCTICA IS A DESERT

So little rain or snow falls in the Antarctic that it is classified as a desert. It is cold and windy and most of its water is locked in ice. In fact, it contains 90 percent of all the ice on the planet.

ANTARCTICA IS THE FIFTH LARGEST CONTINENT, BIGGER THAN EUROPE OR AUSTRALIA.

Continent or not?

Antarctica is the southernmost continent, sitting in the Antarctic Circle. It is a solid landmass that is almost entirely covered by an ice shelf. By contrast, there is no Arctic "continent," but an ocean containing many floating ice caps and various islands belonging to different nations. Both are alarmingly cold, but Antarctica easily takes the trophy for the coldest and driest place on Earth. Its average temperature is -67°F (-55°C).

Humpback whales feed on krill around the coasts of Antarctica.

Hostile land

The continent nearly doubles in size in winter when the coastal waters freeze. Marine birds and mammals such as penguins, seals, and whales make their home in its icy waters, but no vertebrates live on the continent's interior. There are hardly any plants to sustain life, although certain algae turn the snow pink, red, orange, or green in patches.

Snowstorms

A range of mountains divides Antarctica into two parts, east and west. The ice averages 1.2 miles (2 km) thick on the eastern side, but can reach depths of over twice that. The interior is the driest, receiving only 2 inches (5 cm) of snow each year. There is slightly more snowfall around the coast. Strong, fast winds sweep up the snow into storms which block out the sky.

Really remote

Antarctica was the last continent to be discovered, in 1820. It took until 1911 for explorers to trek across it to the South Pole. It still has no permanent residents, but scientists visit for weeks or months to carry out research, and thousands of tourists gain special permission to visit on cruise ships each year. They travel across the ice on motor-powered sleds, as no dogs (or any other non-native species) are allowed there.

LESS THAN HALF A PERCENT OF ANTARCTICA'S LAND IS ICE-FREE.

FACT 6 THERE ARE ENORMOUS SAND DUNES IN EUROPE

The Dune of Pilat in France is the tallest sand dune in Europe, reaching nearly 360 feet (110 m) above sea level. Like many sand dunes, it is on the move, shifting about 16 feet (5 m) a year as sand is blown by the wind.

A wealth of choice

As a continent, Europe contains a wide variety of cultures, languages, and even climate types. It is home to the largest country of all, Russia, which takes up 40 percent of Europe's land area. It also has the world's smallest country, Vatican City, which is only 0.2 square mile (0.44 sq km), and smallest country with a coastline, Monaco. Despite its small size, Europe is the world's richest continent, with a third of the world's wealth.

EUROPE IS THE SECOND SMALLEST OF THE CONTINENTS, BUT HAS THE THIRD LARGEST POPULATION.

Russia's capital, Moscow, is in the European part of the country.

A land divided

Geographers have discussed the boundaries between Europe and Asia for centuries, as both sit side by side on one landmass. A commonly used border (dividing line) runs down the Caucasus and Ural mountain ranges. This means that several countries (Georgia, Azerbaijan, Armenia, Turkey, and Russia) sit across two continents. The largest part of Russia is in Asia, but about 77% of the population lives in the European part.

Happy days

Northern Europe has cold winters with few hours of daylight. Despite that, these countries (Denmark, Norway, Iceland, Finland, and Sweden) score highly in the world's happiness ratings. Southern European countries sit on the Mediterranean and enjoy mild winters and hot summers. A band of Central European countries in between are characterized by picturesque mountain scenery, wide rivers, and large areas of agriculture.

Forest and ocean

After the last ice age, most of Europe was covered in forest, and that is reflected in its wildlife even today. Animals such as bears, badgers, foxes, deer, wild boar, squirrels, and lynxes make their home here. The North Sea has around 230 species of fish such as cod, haddock, herring, and mackerel, while the Mediterranean contains over twice that number—about 7 percent of the global total of marine species, including bream, sea bass, sardines, and mullet.

GREECE HAS OVER 200 INHABITED ISLANDS, WITH MANY FISHERMEN LIVING THERE.

FACT 7 90% OF ALL RICE IS EATEN IN ASIA

Nearly half of the world's population of 7 billion eat rice on a regular basis. Yet more than 90 percent of the total grown on the planet is consumed in a single continent.

ON MOUNTAINOUS LAND, RICE IS GROWN IN TERRACES. THIS METHOD OF FARMING HELPS TO PREVENT FLOODS AND LANDSLIDES.

Record breakers

Asia is the biggest continent, both in area and the number of inhabitants. Nearly two thirds of the world's people live in Asia, even though the continent is only one third of the world's landmass. It contains the world's highest point (Mount Everest) and lowest point (the Dead Sea), and has the longest coastline of any continent. Asia stretches from Turkey in the west to Siberia in the east.

ASIA IS THE ONLY CONTINENT WITH TIGERS LIVING IN THE WILD.

Climate changes

Nearly all of Asia sits in the northern hemisphere. Of course, being so vast, it has many different climate types. Its most northerly areas have extremely cold winters, while countries in the south are hot all year round. Southeast Asia, trapped between the Indian and Pacific oceans, attracts many tourists, drawn to its idyllic beaches, hours of sunshine, and fascinating cultures.

Special residents

Such a huge continent is bound to have a wide variety of creatures. Asia has its own iconic species, such as tigers, Indian elephants, giant pandas, king cobras, orangutans, and Komodo dragons. It is also home to less well-known species such as dugongs, tarsiers, gibbons, Bactrian camels, and slow lorises. The distinctive peacock with its splendid tail originally came from India, Pakistan, and Sri Lanka.

High up

China's mountains aren't as tall as others in Asia, but some are equally breathtaking. Candy-striped in a rainbow of red, blue, and yellow, the Danxia range was formed from compressed sandstone over 20 million years ago. Far over on the west of the continent, the Ural Mountains form a natural border with Europe.

DANXIA MEANS "ROSY CLOUD," AND AT SUNRISE AND SUNSET, THE DANXIA MOUNTAINS SEEM TO GLOW.

FACT 8 THE MOON CAN MAKE RAINBOWS

A rainbow is caused by light passing through water droplets. Moonlight can make a rainbow, although moonbows are much rarer and paler than those created by sunlight.

THE BEST MOONBOWS APPEAR WHEN THE MOON IS FULL AND LOW IN THE SKY.

African gems

This moonbow (below) is made by the moonlight passing through spray from Victoria Falls, on the Zambezi River between Zambia and Zimbabwe in southern Africa. It is one of the places best known for seeing moonbows. Victoria Falls is classified as the largest waterfall in the world as it is both wide and high, creating an enormous sheet of falling water. Africa is also home to the world's largest desert, the Sahara, and longest river, the Nile.

The Great Mosque of Djenné in Mali is made of mud bricks.

A taste of the north

Africa is the second-largest continent and is divided in two by the Sahara Desert. Countries to the north are strongly linked to the Mediterranean countries in southern Europe and the Arab states of the Middle East. Their climate suits a wide range of crops such as lemons, oranges, dates, olives, and figs, which are often used in the region's cooking.

Rich and poor

There are riches hidden in the African landscape—literally. More than 40% of the world's gold reserves are here, and 90% of platinum, plus copper, tin, uranium, emeralds, and diamonds. However, Africa is also the poorest continent, with 75% of the world's poorest countries. Approximately 1 in 3 people are undernourished and over 400 million people live in extreme poverty, on less than $1.25 a day.

Southern safaris

Several of the countries south of the Sahara Desert are famous for their safaris to see Africa's most sought-after animals. Uganda and Rwanda are home to gorillas and chimps; Namibia and Botswana have cheetahs, zebras, leopards, giraffes, and hippos; while Kenya's Masai Mara reserve and South Africa's Kruger Park are noted for the "Big Five"—elephants, rhinos, buffalo, leopards, and lions. If it's big cats you're after, try Tanzania. It has more lions than the other safari nations put together!

AN AFRICAN ELEPHANT HAS TWO "FINGERS" ON ITS TRUNK, WHICH CAN BE USED TO PICK UP ITEMS AS SMALL AS A GRAIN OF RICE.

FACT 9 ROCKS CAN MOVE BY THEMSELVES!

Large rocks mysteriously slide along the floor of places such as Death Valley, leaving trails behind them. Scientists only discovered the cause of the motion in 2014.

National treasure

Using video, time-lapse photography, and GPS tracking, the scientists finally solved the mystery of the sailing stones. They are pushed along in ice sheets that break up in the sunshine. So many things about Death Valley are remarkable, from its position as the lowest, hottest, driest place in the U.S. to its salt flats and sand dunes, meteor crater, and mountain peaks with snow on top. Death Valley is the largest national park in the lower 48 states, and some of its rocks are over 1.7 billion years old!

FACT 10

Canada and the U.S. are the biggest countries in North America, and the second and third biggest in the world.

GEOLOGISTS STUDYING THE MOVING STONES NAMED THEM ALL, WITH THE BIGGEST NAMED KAREN!

The Blue Hole is an underwater cave off the coast of Belize.

Limited languages

North America is the third largest of the continents, and includes the islands of the Caribbean plus Mexico, Guatemala, Belize, Honduras, El Salvador, Nicaragua, Costa Rica, and Panama. North America is unusual since only three main languages dominate: English, Spanish (largely in the south), and French (in Canada and the Caribbean). Mexico has more speakers of Spanish than any other country, including Spain.

Hunting and farming

Much of the land in North America was colonized in the 15th and 16th centuries by European settlers, but native people lived there long before this. Many of them in the north were hunters, while in the south, three great farming civilizations dominated: the Aztec, Maya, and Inca. They had powerful rulers, complex governments and cultures, and intriguing religions with many gods, temples, pyramids, and even sacrifices.

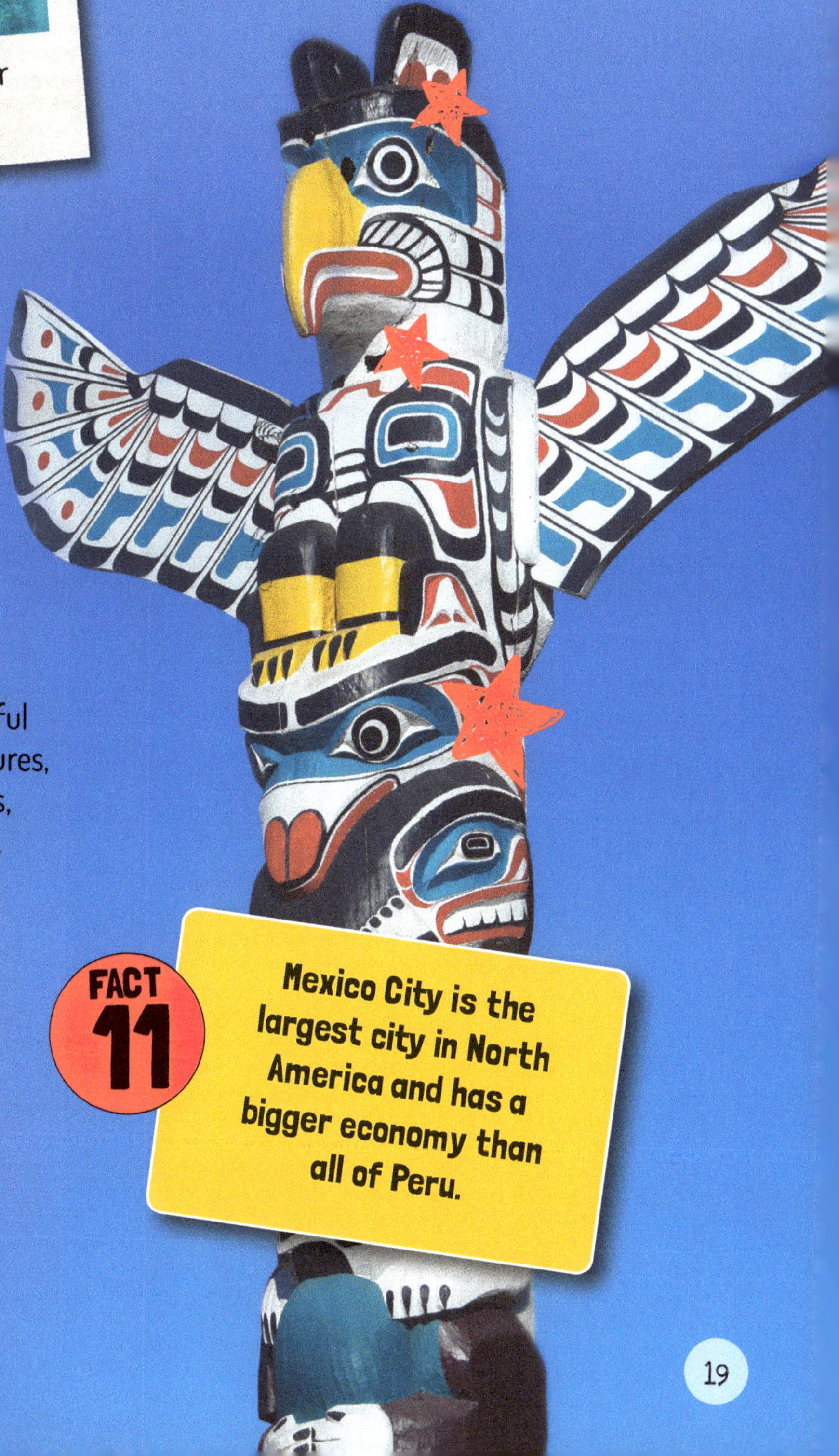

Land, air, and sea

Every type of habitat can be found across North America, from tundra and coral reefs to deserts and rain forests. Its oceans teem with sharks, whales, and dolphins, and its mountains are home to wolves, bears, and cougars. Even its skies are full, and mighty birds of prey such as vultures, eagles, and condors thrive.

FACT 11

Mexico City is the largest city in North America and has a bigger economy than all of Peru.

FACT 12 THERE'S A TRAIN AT THE END OF THE WORLD

Ushuaia in South America is the southernmost city on Earth, and is often referred to as "El Fin del Mundo" or the End of the World. The steam train there is the farthest south on the planet.

THE SOUTHERN END OF SOUTH AMERICA IS KNOWN AS PATAGONIA, AND MANY PEOPLE THERE CAN SPEAK WELSH!

High and dry

Most of South America is in the southern hemisphere. It has the Atlantic Ocean on its east side, and the Pacific Ocean on the other, with the mighty Andes mountain range running down the west coast. In the north, the Amazon river basin, containing the largest rain forest on the planet, covers an area the size of the United States. The continent also boasts the highest waterfall (Angel Falls in Venezuela) and the driest desert (the Atacama in Chile).

Big, big Brazil

South America is the fourth largest continent by size, and fifth largest by population. It has only 12 countries, with Brazil by far the largest. It covers nearly half of the continent! Nearly all the people living in South America speak Spanish or Portuguese, a legacy of the European conquistadores who claimed the lands for their mother countries.

This modern cathedral is in Brasília, Brazil's capital.

In exchange

Many new discoveries were carried back to Europe from South America, including pineapples, potatoes, chili peppers, maize, sunflowers, peanuts, and chocolate. In exchange, the Europeans introduced horses, cattle, sheep, pigs, farming equipment, and unfortunately, nonnative diseases that spread as epidemics because the local people had no immunity against them.

THE AMAZON RIVER USED TO BE A VAST INLAND SEA, AND STILL CONTAINS STINGRAYS!

High-altitude animals

The Amazon rain forest has an astonishing array of indigenous creatures (ones that occur naturally in that habitat), but the Andes Mountains also have their own exclusive animals. The vicuña and guanaco are wild relatives of llamas and alpacas and are adapted to life at very high altitudes. The mountains also have one of the highest diversity of amphibians (frogs, toads, and salamanders) in the world.

FACT 13 AUSTRALIA IS WIDER THAN THE MOON

The moon's diameter is about 2,100 miles (3,380 km), while Australia measures roughly 2,485 miles (4,000 km) across. It is entirely surrounded by ocean, making it the world's largest island. Except... it isn't.

The island continent

Strictly speaking, Australia is an island, but it is so large it is considered to be a continent, not an island. Australia sits on its own tectonic plate and has a very distinct culture and types of plants and animals. It has more than 8,000 islands around it, including New Zealand, New Guinea, and thousands of small Pacific islands. The continent is home to a host of species that are not found anywhere else in the world, particularly marsupials.

FACT 14 People have lived in Australia for around 50,000 years, making their indigenous society the oldest on the planet.

THE PLATYPUS IS FOUND ONLY IN AUSTRALIA, AND HAS A POISONOUS SPIKE ON ITS HIND FOOT.

Kata Tjuta is a collection of sacred rocks in the Australian Outback.

Seeing red

Most of Australia's inhabitants live around the edge of the continent. Its largest cities are Sydney, Melbourne, and Brisbane in the east, and Perth on the west coast. The huge interior of the landmass has few people living there, and is known as the Outback. Much of it is dry, flat, and rocky, with red-rock monoliths in places, such as the famous Uluru.

FACT 15

The world's longest fence runs over 3,400 miles (5,500 km) across southeastern Australia to stop wild dingoes from attacking farm animals.

Watch out!

Australia is famous for having many of the world's most dangerous animals. Venomous snakes such as the taipan, death adder, tiger snake, and brown snake live alongside deadly spiders such as the funnel web spider and redback. Crocodiles and sharks also have a fearsome reputation. The oceans are home to lethal stonefish, blue-ringed octopus, and the box jellyfish, whose sting can kill a human in minutes.

THE FIRST COMMERCIAL BUNGEE JUMPS TOOK PLACE IN AUCKLAND IN 1986.

Eastern island

New Zealand is around 28 times smaller than Australia but equally fascinating. Its capital, Wellington, is the southernmost capital in the world. Farm animals outnumber people by around 9 to 1, and the country is so narrow that nowhere on the mainland is more than 75 miles (120km) from the ocean. With many mountains and fjords, it is not surprising that New Zealand is home to the bungee jump. Spectacular glaciers, geysers, volcanoes, forests, and beaches can also be found in the country.

FACT 16 SUNSET IS BEFORE SUNRISE IN ICELAND!

Iceland chooses to be in a different time zone from the one its position on the planet would suggest. That, added to its extremely long summer days, means that the sun sets before it rises

Clock confusion

Sunset is so late in summer near the Arctic Circle that it slips into the following day. For a couple of weeks in Reykjavik, Iceland, the sun sets after midnight, in the very early hours of the morning. It rises again a few hours later the same day.

THE TIME WHEN THE SUN IS AT ITS HIGHEST IN THE SKY IS KNOWN AS SOLAR NOON.

Time zones

Lines of longitude help locate places on Earth's surface. These lines are also used to standardize time. The 0 line passes through Greenwich, UK, and places to the east and west of this change time by 1-hour jumps as you move farther away: if it is noon in Greenwich, it's 7 a.m. in New York. However, these time zones don't always sit comfortably with the sun's position in the sky. Solar noon can be hours away from noon on the clock!

JAPAN IS FARTHER EAST THAN VLADIVOSTOK IN RUSSIA, BUT ITS TIME IS TWO HOURS BEHIND RUSSIAN TIME.

Drawing a line

Time zones don't follow longitude lines exactly. They zigzag to follow geographical borders. Many west African nations that lie due south of the UK are in the same time zone as Greenwich, but Algeria, which sits across the 0 longitude line, stays one hour ahead to avoid confusion within the country.

Washington, D.C., is three hours ahead of the west coast of the U.S.

Lands divided

Very large nations are split into several time zones; the U.S. has six, from Hawaii in the far west across to Florida in the east. However, some countries choose to work to the same time zone across the whole country. Geographically, China should be divided into five time zones, but the government keeps it all on Beijing time. That means that sunset in the far west might occur at midnight.

EVEN MORE FACTS!

You've found out a lot about continents, but there's always more to discover! Boost your knowledge with these 10 quick facts.

The largest continent is Asia, with an area of just over 17 million square miles (44 million sq km). The smallest continent is Australia, which covers 2.9 million square miles (7.7 million sq km).

Antarctica's ice contains about the same amount of water as the Atlantic Ocean.

The Atacama Desert is the driest place in the world, with some parts receiving less than 1 mm of rain each year. The only things able to live there are microscopic organisms.

Europe was home to the ancient civilizations of Greece and Rome, which were the birthplace of democracy.

Asia is the only continent that is connected to two other continents, Europe and Africa. In the winter, when ice forms over the Bering Sea, it joins up with a third continent, North America.

There are 2,138 different languages spoken across Africa, which closely follows Asia in having the biggest number. North and South America have half this amount, at 1,064 languages, while Europe only has 286.

Greenland is the biggest island on Earth, and the least densely populated country. A thick sheet of ice covers the center of the country, so most people live on the west coast.

North and South America were named after the Italian explorer Amerigo Vespucci, who between 1501–1502 proved that Brazil and the West Indies were not part of Asia, but a separate landmass.

The kangaroo is a marsupial that is indigenous to Australia, and one of the country's national symbols. The kangaroo's long, powerful legs and tail help it to travel long distances to find food in a dry, infertile country with unpredictable weather.

All the lines of longitude meet at the North Pole, which means it is in no time zone. If you stood at the North Pole, everywhere you looked would point south.

CONTINENTS GLOSSARY

algae A type of plant with no stems or leaves that grows in water or on damp surfaces.

bungee jump A jump made by someone from a high bridge or building, secured only by a rubber cord attached to the ankles.

colonized Turned into a colony, a country controlled by another, more powerful country.

condense Change from gas into liquid.

conquistadores Spanish conquerors of Central and South America in the sixteenth century.

continental drift The theory that Earth's continents move very slowly over the surface of the planet, toward and away from each other.

economy The wealth that a country or place gets from business and industry.

epidemics Diseases that spread very quickly and affect large numbers of people.

fossil The hard remains of a prehistoric animal or plant found inside a rock.

geologists People who study geology, the study of the Earth's structure, surface, and origins.

habitat The natural environment in which an animal or plant lives.

humidity The amount of water in the air.

ice caps Thick layers of ice and snow that cover the North and South Poles.

ice sheets Large, thick areas of ice, especially those that have existed for a long time.

immunity The ability to resist disease.

indigenous People or things that come from the place where they are found.

inhabited Lived in.

landmass A large and continuous area of land, not interrupted by seas or islands.

lines of longitude Imaginary lines on a map indicating the distance to the west or east from a line passing through Greenwich, UK.

marine Having to do with the sea, or to animals and plants that live in the sea.

marsupials Animals such as kangaroos and koalas. Female marsupials carry their babies in a pouch on their stomach.

mid-ocean ridge An underwater mountain range, formed when two tectonic plates meet at a boundary.

molten A material that has turned to liquid due to very high temperatures.

monoliths A very large, upright piece of stone, especially one that was put in place in ancient times.

NASA An abbreviation for "National Aeronautics and Space Administration." NASA is the American government organization concerned with space travel.

New World A term used to refer to the continents of North and South America.

non-native Animals or plants that do not originate from a place.

northern hemisphere Half of the globe that lies north of the equator.

radar technology The use of high-frequency radio pulses transmitted and reflected back to a transmitter to detect the position of something.

rift valley A long, narrow valley that is the result of the sinking of land between two faults in Earth's plates. The East African Rift Valley is one example.

seafloor spreading This happens at the bottom of an ocean when two tectonic plates move apart and new oceanic crust is formed, which slowly moves away from the ridge.

CONTINENTS GLOSSARY continued

settlers People who go to live in a new country.

solar To do with the sun.

southern hemisphere Half of the globe that lies south of the equator.

species A class of plants or animals that share the same main characteristics and are able to breed with each other.

Spinosaurus A dinosaur, whose name means "spine lizard," that lived in what is now North Africa during the Cretaceous Period, about 112–93.5 million years ago.

tectonic plates Pieces of the Earth's lithosphere, made up of the crust and upper part of the mantle.

time zone One of the areas into which the world is divided, where the time is calculated as being a particular number of hours behind or ahead of the line of longitude marked 0. The line 0 runs through Greenwich, UK.

Triassic Period A period of time lasting 50.6 million years, from the end of the Permian Period 251.9 million years ago to the beginning of the Jurassic Period 201.3 million years ago.

undernourished Weak and unhealthy as a result of not eating enough food, or the right kind of food.

venemous Poisonous.

vertebrates Animals with a backbone.

FURTHER INFORMATION

BOOKS

Brake, Mark. *The Big Earth Book*. London, UK: Lonely Planet Kids, 2017.

Cullis, Megan. *The Usborne Book of Planet Earth*. London, UK: Usborne, 2019.

DK. *DKfindout! Earth*. London, UK: DK, 2017.

DK. *Earth: The Definitive Visual Guide*. London, UK: DK, 2013.

DK. *Pocket Eyewitness Earth: Facts at Your Fingertips*. London, UK: DK, 2018.

Gallagher, Belinda. *Wild About Planet Earth*. Thaxted, UK: Miles Kelly, 2019.

MacDonald, Fiona, and Rupert Matthews. *100 Facts Extreme Earth*. Thaxted, UK: Miles Kelly, 2017.

WEBSITES

CoolKidFacts

https://www.coolkidfacts.com/earth-science/

Discover all sorts of facts about planet Earth, from deserts and mountains to the different types of rocks on our planet. Includes simple science experiments and activity worksheets.

Ducksters Earth Science for Kids

https://www.ducksters.com/science/earth_science/

Head to this website to find out all there is to know about planet Earth; you can also try an earth science crossword puzzle and word search!

Science4Fun

http://science4fun.info/earth-science/

Find out more about planet Earth's geology, meteorology, paleontology, and oceanography.

Publisher's note to educators and parents: Our editors have carefully reviewed these websites to ensure that they are suitable for students. Many websites change frequently, however, and we cannot guarantee that a site's future contents will continue to meet our high standards of quality and educational value. Be advised that students should be closely supervised whenever they access the Internet.

INDEX